Seymour Simon

READERS

PLEASE RETURN TO:
MISS WHITE

D0462647

INCREDIBLE SHARKS

SCHOLASTIC INC.
NEW YORK · TORONTO · LONDON · AUCKLAND · SYDNEY
MEXICO CITY · NEW DELHI · HONG KONG · BUENOS AIRES

Front cover photograph: A sand tiger shark
Title page: A great white shark
Pages 2–3: A school of hammerhead sharks

This book is for my granddaughter Chloe and my grandson Jeremy.

Special thanks to reading consultant Dr. Linda B. Gambrell, Director, School of Education, Clemson University. Dr. Gambrell has served as President of the National Reading Conference and Board Member of the International Reading Association.

Permission to use the following photographs is gratefully acknowledged:
Front cover: © Jeff Rotman/Photo Researchers, Inc.; title page, pages 24–25: © C & M Fallows/Seapics.com; pages 2–3: © Eiichi Kurasawa/Photo Researchers, Inc.; pages 4–5: © Calvert Marine Museum; pages 6–7, 30–31: © David B. Fleetham/Visuals Unlimited; pages 8–9, 22–23, and back cover: © Carl Roessler; pages 10–11: © Jonathan Bird/ORG; pages 14–15: © James D. Watt/Visuals Unlimited; pages 16–17: © David Wrobel/Visuals Unlimited; pages 18–19: © Doug Perrine/Seapics.com; pages 20–21: © Mark Jones/Minden Pictures; pages 26–27: © Richard Herrmann/Visuals Unlimited; pages 28–29: © Tom Campbell/MercuryPress.com; page 32: © Steve Drogin/Seapics.com

No part of this publication may be reproduced in whole or in part, or stored in a retrieval system, or transmitted in any form or by any means, electronic, mechanical, photocopying, recording, or otherwise, without written permission of the publisher. For information regarding permission, write to North-South Books, Inc., 11 East 26th Street, 17th floor, New York, NY 10010.

ISBN 0-439-56095-0

Text copyright © 2003 by Seymour Simon. All rights reserved.
Published by Scholastic Inc., 557 Broadway, New York, NY 10012,
by arrangement with North-South Books, Inc.
SCHOLASTIC and associated logos are trademarks and/or
registered trademarks of Scholastic Inc.

12 11 10 9 8 7 6 5 4   3 4 5 6 7 8/0

Printed in the U.S.A.   23

First Scholastic printing, October 2003

The first sharks lived more than 100 million years before the dinosaurs. The megalodon shark of early times was bigger than a school bus.

The Ultimate Shark

Sharks don't have any bones
in their bodies.
Their skeletons are made of
easy-to-bend cartilage.
It is just like the cartilage you
have in your nose and your ears.

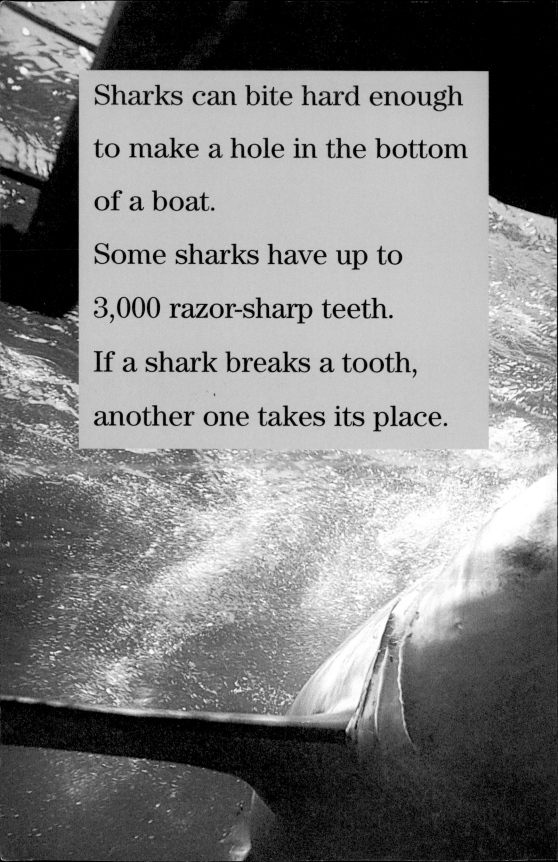

Sharks can bite hard enough to make a hole in the bottom of a boat.

Some sharks have up to 3,000 razor-sharp teeth. If a shark breaks a tooth, another one takes its place.

Sharks don't chew.
They swallow each bite whole.
After a shark has a meal,
it may go for weeks
before it eats again.

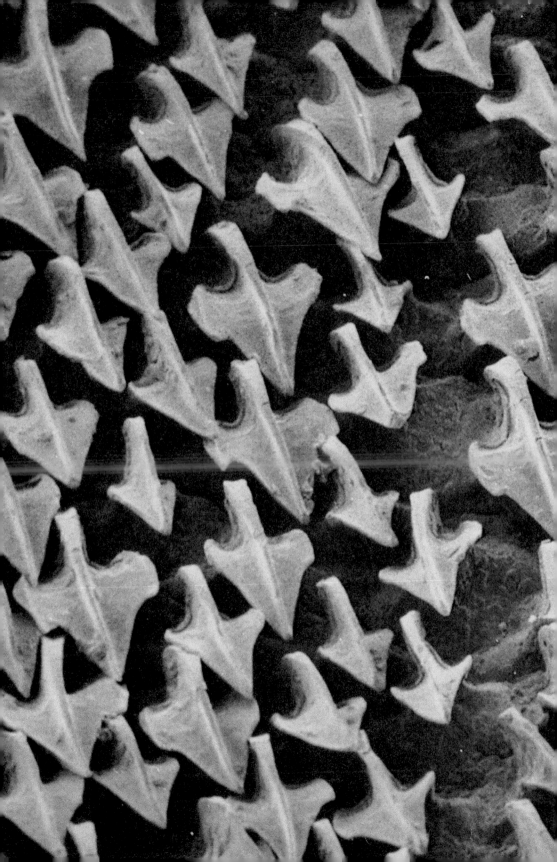

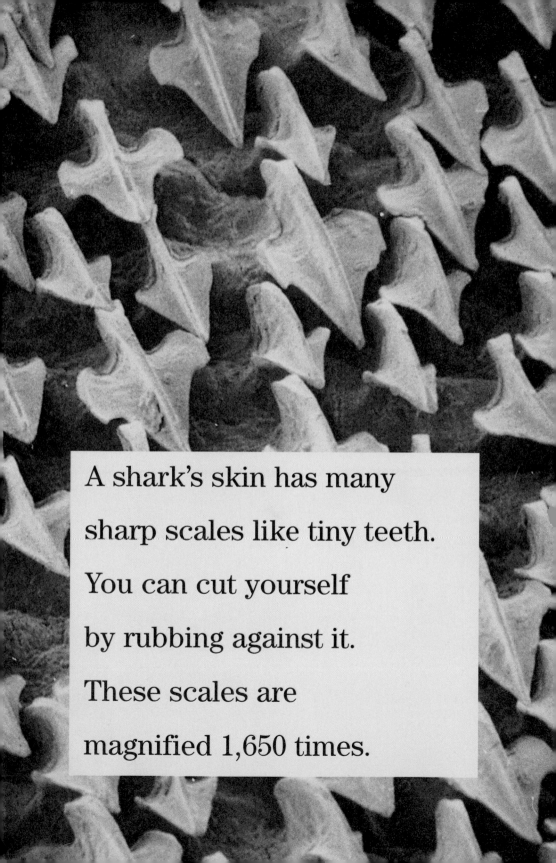

A shark's skin has many
sharp scales like tiny teeth.
You can cut yourself
by rubbing against it.
These scales are
magnified 1,650 times.

Sharks can hear sounds in the water half a mile away.

They can smell even a single drop of blood in the water from more than a mile away.

There are about 400 kinds
of sharks.
Most of them are just
a few feet long.

The whale shark is the biggest, sometimes reaching 50 feet long. Pygmy sharks are only seven or eight inches in length. This wobbegong shark is about four feet long.

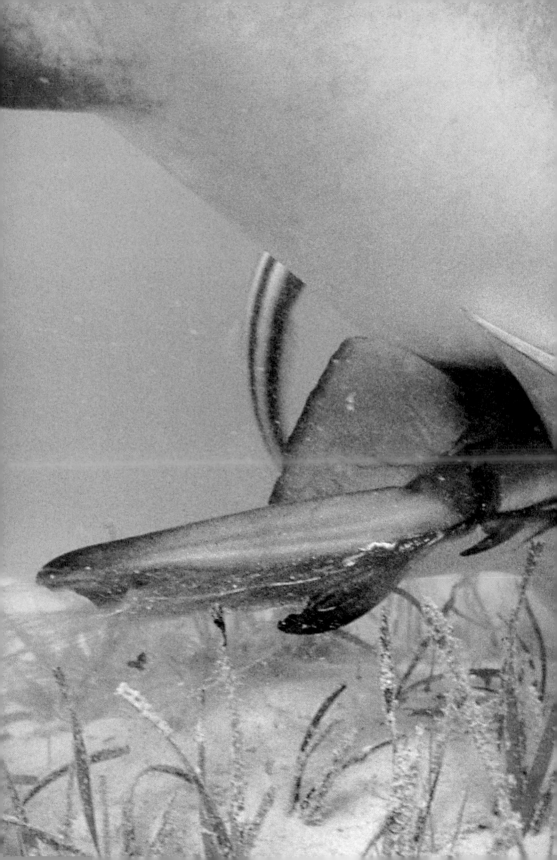

Most sharks are born live,
ready to hunt for food.
Some sharks hatch out of eggs
laid in shells or cases
on the ocean floor.
Baby sharks are called pups.
Blue sharks can give birth to
over 100 pups at one time.

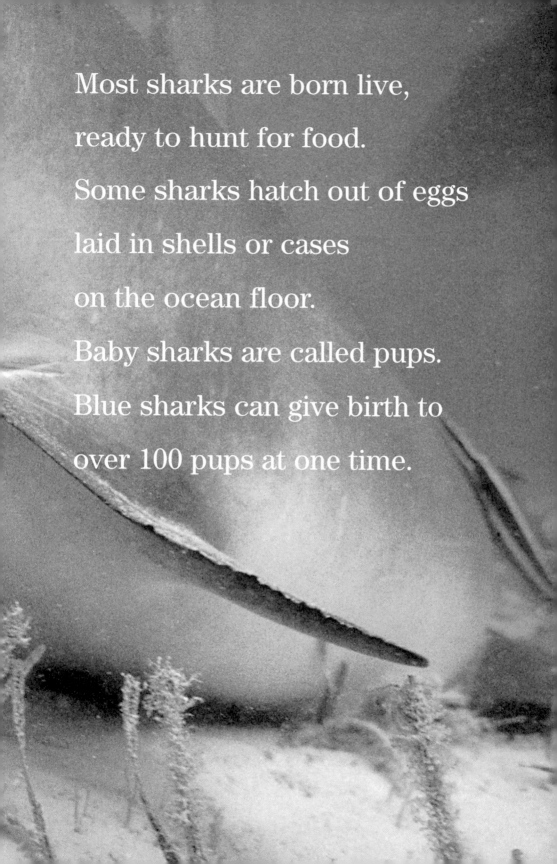

Hammerhead sharks have a wide, thick head that looks like a hammer. Large hammerheads are up to 20 feet long.

The whale shark is the

biggest fish in the seas.

It can weigh as much

as three elephants.

Its six-foot mouth filters
tiny animals and plants
from the water.

The scariest shark is
the great white.
Its jaws are filled with
50 two-and-one-half-inch
sharp teeth.

Its favorite food is seals
or sea lions, not people.

Mako sharks and blue sharks
are the fastest.
They swim faster than
you can run.

Sharks will eat all sorts of strange things they find in the water.

Barrels of nails, cases of wine, shoes, and musical instruments have been found in the stomachs of sharks.

Sharks do not usually
attack people.
Many more people are killed
by insect bites every year
than by sharks.
But people should not swim
in water where sharks
have been seen.

More than 30 different kinds of sharks are found each year.

New facts about sharks are being discovered all the time.